AROUND
MELBOURNE

YARRA VALLEY · MORNINGTON PENINSULA · GEELONG · MACEDON · SUNBURY

TRAVELLING AUSTRALIA'S WINE REGIONS

AROUND
MELBOURNE

YARRA VALLEY • MORNINGTON PENINSULA • GEELONG • MACEDON • SUNBURY

PHOTOGRAPHY BY
R. IAN LLOYD

TEXT BY RITA ERLICH

EDITED BY WENDY MOORE

R. IAN LLOYD PRODUCTIONS

TRAVELLING AUSTRALIA'S WINE REGIONS

CONTENTS

CHAPTER ONE

HISTORY

Australia's first great international diva, Nellie Melba *(opposite)*, for whom the renowned chef Escoffier invented peach Melba and a special kind of toast, sent this photograph, taken in Paris in 1890, home to her father, David Mitchell. She chose the stage-name Melba in honour of her hometown of Melbourne.

Lucky city, Melbourne. The capital of Victoria lies within a charmed circle, surrounded by its food and its holidays. Unusually, for a city of this size, within an hour or two's drive are cattle, sheep, orchards, vegetables, sea and surf, forests and national parks. And, even more unusual for such a city, it has five distinct vineyard regions within easy reach: Yarra Valley, Mornington Peninsula, Geelong, Macedon Ranges and Sunbury.

The vine could be the city symbol for Melbourne: long-lived, productive, an occasion for the exercise of artistic, scientific and technological skills. Victoria has more vineyards and wineries than any other Australian state, and a high proportion of them are within the five areas in the charmed circle. They number in the hundreds, and most are open to the public for cellar-door sales. They grow grapes, they make wine, and they also provide employment and tourism destinations. No wonder Melbourne was chosen as one of the first Global Wine Network Capitals, along with Bordeaux and Florence.

Port Phillip, the great bay around which Melbourne curls, has been known to Europeans since 1803 when an ill-fated convict camp was established near Sorrento on the Mornington Peninsula. A year earlier, the French explorer Nicholas Baudin had met the English navigator Matthew Flinders in Bass Strait. French Island was named as a result of their friendly exchange in Western Port, which is actually on the eastern side of the Peninsula.

Flinders had anchored in Dromana Bay, and climbed to the top of Arthurs Seat, which would have afforded the same geographic view as today with the great sweep of the Peninsula, the Otway ranges in the west, and the distinctive peaks of the You Yangs to the north.

The attraction of the area around Melbourne was not its early urban life. What brought the first European settlers here—across land from New South Wales, and by water from Tasmania—was the search for pastoral land for sheep and cattle. The overland journeys usually had a great and terrible impact on the local Aboriginal tribes, but not all the meetings were murderous. There are records of early encounters on the Mornington Peninsula where there was dancing, not fighting.

John Batman, one of an eager group of investors from Tasmania, acquired Melbourne from the elders of the Wurrundjeri tribe for nominal trinkets. He had come from Tasmania,

An early watercolour, painted in 1855, shows a property known as The Blair in the Yarra Valley. There were many Swiss working in the Yarra Valley at that time, but only British subjects could purchase land.

travelled to the head of Port Phillip Bay, and disembarked on the riverbank, near where the Museum of Immigration now so fittingly stands. William Buckley, a convict who had escaped from Sorrento in 1802 and spent decades living with Aboriginal clans, acted as negotiator between the tribal groups and the white settlers. As a result, John Batman pardoned Buckley.

Batman's words on disembarking are well known: "This is the place for a village," he declared. But it quickly outgrew that description. Within three years, the village and its surrounds was big and lively enough to require a superintendent. Within a few more years, during the 1840s, the politics and economics of European countries caused many to leave their homelands and come to the new world of Australia in search of more promising lives.

Vines and grapes were always part of the promise. The wine industry began bright and bold in Victoria, closely following permanent European settlement. Melbourne was established

in 1835, and three years later the first vineyard was planted in the Yarra Valley. Just over a generation after the first vines were planted, The Age newspaper was waving the flag for Victorian wines, distinguishing them from the vintages of Sydney and South Australia, and urging Government action in enabling wines to be sold more easily.

The leading article in December 1863 argued that locally made wines should be "the daily beverage of the people", and that the Legislature should get on with making them profitably so. A month later, the newspaper published the first article in a series on Victorian vineyards, starting with those around Geelong. The series was never completed, but it ran for long enough to give a good picture of the vigour of the early winemaking days.

At the heart of wine's success was a woman named Sophie, wife of Charles Joseph La Trobe, the first superintendent of Port Phillip district, and later the first governor of the state of Victoria. An Englishman of Huguenot descent, he had been educated in Switzerland where he met and married Sophie de Montmollin of Neuchatel in 1835.

La Trobe's British colonial career began in the West Indies, after which he was sent to the Port Phillip district, as the southern part of Victoria was then known. At that stage in the La Trobes' lives, it was probably not considered a great career move. Why would two such well-connected people have accepted the move to such a distant land?

The story starts much earlier, long before Captain John Macarthur established Australia's first commercial winery in the 1820s at Camden

Park, his property in New South Wales. (He is regarded as one of the founders of the Australian wine industry along with Gregory Blaxland and James Busby.) When Macarthur was summoned back to England after his disputes with Governor Bligh, and was forbidden to return before 1817, he spent much time travelling on the continent. Meanwhile, his Australian-born son, William, went to school in Vevey, Switzerland, where his best mate was Count Louis de Pourtalès of Neuchatel, Sophie's cousin. It is said that the Count encouraged Sophie to go to distant Australia because he had grown up with William Macarthur's stories.

It is unlikely that Sophie La Trobe sent encouraging post cards from her new home. But when the daughter of a distinguished Neuchatel family went to a foreign land, her presence was a welcoming beacon, especially during troubled times at home. In 1840, within months of her arrival, a number of Neuchatelois had arrived, some with the express purpose of planting vineyards. It was the start of an immigration chain: the Delperroud brothers came first, followed by members of the Dardel, Pettavel, Brequet, Niffennecker, Cornu and Deppler families. After the brief but unpleasant civil war in Switzerland came Sophie's nephew, Adolphe de Meuron-Osterwald, then Paul de Castella, and Guillaume and Samuel de Pury (more of Sophie's nephews), and Clement Deschamps and his brothers.

Many of these names are still evident. Pettavel is the same given to a restaurant and winery near Geelong (where so many of the early immigrants settled to cultivate their vineyards). Deschamps Avenue is in the heart of Lilydale.

The avenue of trees that Paul de Castella planted for his bride in 1853 still stands at Yering Station, while the de Pury family continues to live in the Yarra Valley.

The Swiss were not alone in their enthusiasm for the vine and its fruit. In those early days, winemaking was remarkably popular. There were vineyards all through areas that are now Melbourne suburbs—Moonee Ponds, Flemington, Tooronga, Camberwell, Ivanhoe, even in Collins Street in the heart of the city. The present inner-suburban city of Boroondara was particularly favoured for vineyards in the

S. T. Gill (1818 -1880) is best known for his views of the Victorian goldfields, and other aspects of colonial life. This early watercolour, circa 1847, shows an unusual tall trellising system for grapes. By that time, there were hundreds of vineyards in Melbourne, with the Yarra Valley and Geelong emerging as distinct areas.

1860s. Then they gradually disappeared as real estate values rose, and land use changed from viticulture to residential.

The new settlers—Swiss, German, English, Scots, and all the others—made wine because they drank wine. That is why they all planted vineyards with such energy from the 1830s onwards. Perhaps wine was a favoured beverage, like beer and spirits, in the days before reliably clean drinking water. Or, perhaps the absence of decent malted barley for beer-

making turned their minds to wine. Mostly, it seems, being a vigneron was all the rage, much as it is now.

In December 1863, the leading article in *The Age* spelled it out: "The cultivation of the vine is ... not merely a profitable, but a refining pursuit." Wine was work for gentlemen, and every smart gentleman wanted to cultivate vines. Among them were the Hon. R. C. Hope, chairman of committees of the Legislative Council, and David Mitchell, architect, planner,

An early picnic among giant trees and tall ferns in the cool retreat of Mount Macedon in 1868. Picnics must have been popular then, because this wood engraving is one of many showing such scenes during this period.

and father of Australia's first great international diva, Dame Nellie Melba.

When Edward Henty sailed from Tasmania in 1834 to settle in Portland, in southwestern Victoria (thereby becoming the first free European settler in what was to become Victoria), he had vines to plant. But there is no record of how they fared. In 1838, when the Scottish-born Ryrie brothers travelled overland from New South Wales to find grazing country for their cattle, they brought vines with them and planted them at Yering, on the Yarra. Four years after that, the Neuchatel vineyard near Geelong was established. By 1864, according to

a report of the time, that vineyard was planted with "Black Cluster, or Miller's Burgundy, the Hermitage, the Burgundy, the Black Frontignac, the Esparte, the Grenache, and the Pineau noir" among red grapes. The white varieties included "the Chasselas, the Rousset, the Pineau blanc, the Pineau gris, the White Frontignac, the Gouais, and the Sweetwater." The report also tells that while an olive tree flourished, the orange trees did not bear fruit.

In the year that was written, Victoria had been a colony independent of the Colony of New South Wales for 13 years. But in the meantime, something more momentous

In 1873 Geelong's crowds gathered to view the *Cerberus*. She was the strongest armed ship of her day and was stationed in Port Phillip Bay to keep away invaders. She was later sunk at Black Rock as a breakwater and there is currently a campaign afoot to raise her.

occurred. In 1851, gold was discovered at Harcourt, near Ballarat. It changed Melbourne forever: by the 1880s, the city was known as Marvellous Melbourne, and was the richest in the colonies. In 1840, Melbourne's population stood at only 7,000; by 1891 there were half a million inhabitants.

Gold was magic wherever it was found. It had the ability to multiply and diversify the population quite spectacularly, bringing in an endless and hopeful stream of immigrants from all corners of the world. They came from China, the USA, Ireland, England, Scotland and Wales, France, Germany and Italy.

The lucky ones struck gold; the canny ones provided the gold-seekers with provisions, including wine to drink, made from the fruit of burgeoning local vineyards. There was more than one way to strike it rich.

Victorian wines struck it rich, too. The fact that *The Age* newspaper ran a series on Victorian vineyards in 1864 was an indicator of the value of the local product. By then, the wines were doing very nicely in exhibitions at home and abroad.

The 19th-century exhibition was the forerunner of what is now called an Expo —a celebratory, self-congratulatory display of manufacturing, industry, and even the arts. There were colonial, intercolonial, national and international exhibitions in Melbourne and Sydney, often preparatory to much grander affairs in London, Paris, or Vienna. (Crystal Palace was built to house the first International Exhibition in London in 1851.)

From the late 1860s onwards, Victorian wines showed well at exhibitions—including, and especially, the wines from Geelong and other Melbourne districts. At the 1873 Vienna Exhibition, some of the French judges insisted that the fine Hermitage they had sampled must have come from France (shipped to Australia, and back again for the Exhibition), and took some persuading otherwise. As a result of the fine showing of Australian wine, the Acclimatisation Society of Victoria was given a Diploma of Honour.

This historic photograph from the 1890s shows the de Pury family with Aboriginal elder William Barak, who was a distinguished painter and family friend. The de Pury brothers and William Barak shared an interest in painting and a famous portrait of Barak was painted by one of the brothers.

There were triumphs at every exhibition, most notably for the wines that came from the magic circle around Melbourne. Every prize and medal provided an opportunity to wave the flag for the Victorian wine industry and to secure its place in the world in the way envisaged by *The Age* in 1863: "In a few years hence, winegrowing will be the leading occupation throughout the colony, nor shall we hesitate to enter into comparison with the wines of France, Spain and Portugal."

Two highlights from the beginning and the end of the 1880s boom illustrated the euphoria of the times: St Hubert's won the prize of Kaiser Wilhelm I of Germany at the Melbourne International Exhibition of 1880-1881, and Paul de Castella's Yering vineyard won a grand prize in Paris in 1889.

Melbourne's Royal Exhibition Buildings were designed by David Mitchell (father of Dame Nellie Melba) for the big event. At that time, it is estimated there were about 280 hectares of vines in the Yarra Valley alone. It peaked at 404 hectares in 1904, a figure that was not matched again until 1987.

In 1889, when Victoria had 5,100 hectares under vine, Paul de Castella's Yering vineyard won a grand prize in Paris in 1889—one of only seven such prizes, and the only southern hemisphere vineyard to be so favoured. By then, however, the continuing success of the industry was looking decidedly uncertain.

All hands gathered at Yeringberg for this photograph, taken in the 1880s. The property always ran cattle and sheep, even when its wines were winning prizes internationally. The number of workers reflects the size of the farm, including the vineyards.

As is the way of things, the spectacular boom went bust. Each region had its own story of decline, and each in its own time.

Struck by a succession of blows to its vineyards, the once-thriving Geelong region was the first and saddest hit. The worst was phylloxera, an aphid that destroys the roots of vines, discovered in a Geelong district vineyard in 1877. The cure is to plant on American vine rootstock, because American vines are not susceptible. At the time, the entire Australian wine industry was seen to be at risk. Vines were pulled out and burnt; vineyard after vineyard disappeared. In 1892, the Government declared that it was safe to replant—but by then it was too late.

It has been suggested that the Geelong district was not in robust health anyway, because many of the family vineyards were facing the problems of succession. If the children or grandchildren did not want to take over the vineyards, what would become of them? By the 1890s, with Victoria in the grip of Depression, the answer was clear. Not much. In wine terms, it took until the 1960s for a renewal.

Sunbury had gone into decline during the 1880s, as the gentlemen-vignerons discovered that vineyards were not only expensive, with difficulties like drought, but that they themselves lacked management skills. By the late 1880s, it was clear the future was extremely limited. As a result, the land reverted to sheep,

With or without vines, the Mornington Peninsula has always been a popular holiday destination. This 1930s poster by James Northfield was one of many he made for Victorian Railways promoting tourist destinations in the state.

considerably more tolerant of drought, and mixed farming

The Yarra Valley looked in comparatively good shape. But the rest of Melbourne was not. All through the 1880s, there had been a growing anti-alcohol lobby, encouraged particularly by a James Munro, State Premier and president of the Temperance movement (Victorian Alliance for the Suppression of the Liquor Traffic). On its own, this was not a major problem. But then the early 1890s brought a Depression as severe as that of the 1930s — so bad, in fact, that in 1893, many banks closed their doors.

The vignerons of the Yarra might have survived that, as they might have survived the difficulties of succession and finding good workers. But there was a series of other blows, ranging from the site specific (frost) to the national (Federation) and international (World War I).

Frost was known in the Yarra Valley, but it had become worse — perhaps because of further land clearing. Federation was an issue because it ended the state taxes and excises that had protected Victoria's wines on the local market, thus giving South Australian wines a competitive edge. Their vines were more productive because the climate was warmer and more reliable, and they were cheaper. Federation also changed Australia's attitude to immigration: mainly Northern Europeans with preference given to English speakers. It was a far cry from the days of the La Trobes and the polyglot gold rush.

World War I changed Australia in many ways. In wine terms, it meant no labour force (most eligible males were serving overseas), diminished sales (especially with the introduction of six o'clock closing for hotel liquor sales), a diminished export market, and not much appetite for fine wine. The appearance of downy mildew (a vine disease) and starlings (which fly in clouds and devour grapes) did not help, either.

After the War, land in the Yarra Valley was used for more valuable purposes than vineyards — residential sub-divisions, dairy farms and orchards. Vineyards declined all through the 1920s. By the mid-1930s, after the Depression, there were no more vines in the Yarra Valley.

Then, a good generation later, it all started again. The great vineyard revival began in the 1960s, as Australians became increasingly interested in wine, with vineyard areas around Melbourne extending south to the Mornington Peninsula and north to Macedon. In 1960, there were no wineries within coo-ee of Melbourne. Now there are five areas encircling the city in a productive and joyful cordon.

The homestead at Coolart on the Mornington Peninsula *(far left)* and its avenue of trees *(left)* are part of the legacy of this important old farming property. The historic building has been restored and is open to the public. Its gardens provide picnic areas, and the surrounding reconstructed wetlands are a haven for birds and birdwatchers.

Nineteenth-century buildings were built to last. Guill de Pury *(above)* stands in the original winery at Yeringberg that his grandfather built in the 1860s. The building was designed by David Mitchell, father of Dame Nellie Melba, and is a model of winemaking architecture. Grapes were crushed into the railway trolleys and tipped into fermentation vats. The Yarra Glen Grand hotel *(right)*, is an impressive example of boom-time 1880s architecture.

The name of Terminus House at Point Lonsdale *(above)* is a reminder of the old railway line. Built in 1884, it is one of Victoria's oldest guesthouses. The size of the Daylesford Hotel *(right)*, and its position on the corner of the main street, recalls Daylesford's importance in gold-mining days. Miners needed a good pub just as much as modern travellers.

Old homestead properties are still a feature of the landscape. Australind at Flinders *(above)*, with its classic wrap-around verandah providing shelter from sun and rain, was built in the 1880s. The Cape Schanck lighthouse at the southern tip of the Mornington Peninsula *(right)* provided a different kind of protection—its light warning ships of the land mass. The southern coast of Victoria is full of lighthouses, and the waters off the Great Ocean Road are full of the wrecks of ships that failed to see the warnings.

CHAPTER TWO

YARRA VALLEY

The Yarra is Melbourne's river, and like Melbourne's weather, it is a source of many jokes. By the time it reaches the city, it is joke material because it is not quite enough of what is wanted in a river. It is not wide, nor navigable, nor majestic enough. But its presence is the reason that Melbourne was established where it was.

The indigenous Worwurung people called it Yarra Yarra, which meant "ever flowing". The name probably applied to the river, but could equally refer to its course, which takes 245 kilometres for a journey of about 90 kilometres as the crow flies. The Yarra rises in the mountains east of Warburton, and serpentines its way along to Port Phillip Bay. It is in no hurry: it ambles, it wanders, it detours, it curls, it crimps, it breaks off into billabongs.

The Yarra Valley is defined as the catchment area of the Yarra. It's big, but for travelling purposes, is roughly divided into three arms, according to the highways. The Melba Highway runs past Coombe Cottage, where Dame Nellie Melba lived in retirement, and heads north to Yea and into the Great Dividing Range. The Maroondah goes east to Healesville, once a major holiday centre for Melbourne, and into the Divide. The Warburton Highway, the most southerly, runs through the wettest country, and leads to Mount Donna Buang, which provides lots of Melbourne children with their first experience of snow, because it's the closest snowfield to the city.

The Valley's surprisingly diverse geography, climate, botany, and economy are the reasons for its enduring success, and its future. What makes it so special is the mix of big company and small family businesses, of mainstream and niche markets, of river and forest and horticulture, of high-tech winemaking and high-value tourism, all within a short distance of Melbourne.

In the early years of European settlement, the Yarra's enormous pastoral runs provided land for cattle and sheep, with some vines for fun and profit. The Ryrie brothers, who arrived in 1838, ran 17,400 hectares, extending from Woori Yallock in the south to the Yarra River. They called their property Yering, after the local word meaning both a deep pool, and a watering and gathering place. Today, Aboriginal words still provide a wealth of confusion for winery names: Yering Station, Yering Farm, Yarra Yering, Yeringberg, Yarra Edge, Yarra Yarra, Yarra Ridge, Yarra Burn.

The Black Spur near Healesville provides a crossing through the mountain ash forest *(left)*. The trees are remarkably tall and straight, and enable a dense layering of vegetation that feeds and shelters an abundance of wildlife.

Each of these wineries has its own story. Each will lead the visitor on to something else within the Yarra Valley. The attraction for everyone has always been the area's diversity—and its beauty. Hubert de Castella, writing in 1886, described it enthusiastically: "About thirty miles from Melbourne, a basin of some 20,000 acres lies, surrounded by the Dividing ranges on the north and east, by the Plenty Ranges on the west, and by the Dandenong mountain and its spurs on the south. Hills after hills seem as if they had tumbled down from this last mountain, invaded the valley from the open end, and stopped just sufficiently far away from the winding Yarra to display a succession of most romantic landscapes."

The view from the tasting room at Domaine Chandon is good enough to bottle, as is the panorama from the top of Yeringberg. No one has ever tired of the mountain ash forest on Black Spur where trees as tall and straight as columns in a Gothic cathedral, filter and colour the light as surely as any stained glass. There's Myers Creek, Mount Donna Buang, and the Toolangi State Forest: cool rainforest, with mountain ash, blackwood, myrtle beech, sassafras, luscious tree ferns, and all the other life forms they support.

So many shades of blue and green. "They're the colours of the area," says potter David Williams of Toolangi Pottery, whose rare glazes often yield a flowering of crystals that resemble aspects of forest life. "I love all the different greens," he says, referring to the landscape colours, which have attracted visitors for more than a century.

Once there were 70 guesthouses around Healesville, and a good sprinkling around Warburton. At Strathvea, where the last of the original guesthouses still operates, there was once a dairy so guests could enjoy not only clean fresh air, but also fresh milk, cream and butter. In the first part of the 20th century, this area was important dairy country, supplying the growing city of Melbourne.

People often came for their health, and for rest and recreation, but no one then or now would come for the quiet. This part of the country is amazingly noisy with the daily (and nightly) screeches, whoops, whistles, cackles, warbling, twitters and trills of birds, insects and frogs. At Strathvea, there are shrieking peacocks as well as cockatoos, rosellas, lorikeets, magpies, crows, currawongs and kookaburras.

Occasionally, a single bird will create the sounds of all the others, and anything else that's noiseworthy. Lyrebirds are such brilliant mimics that their repertoire might include the sounds of different brands of chain-saw (noises learnt when the timber industry played an important role here) in addition to all the other birds. A lyrebird in Healesville Sanctuary has even perfected the whirr of a film on automatic re-wind—a bravura little performance that always causes tourists to reach for their cameras in bewilderment.

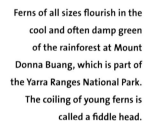

Ferns of all sizes flourish in the cool and often damp green of the rainforest at Mount Donna Buang, which is part of the Yarra Ranges National Park. The coiling of young ferns is called a fiddle head.

A little further south, on the Warburton Highway, glass artist Rob Knottenbelt has identified 40 different species of fungi more or less at his back door, and says that about half of Victoria's frog species are in the area.

"It's cool, it's wet, it's beautiful," he says of the surrounding country. Born in Holland, he grew up in New Zealand and came to Australia originally to study winemaking at Roseworthy in South Australia. Instead, he studied ceramics with potter Milton Moon, and then glass took hold of him. He found the location for his studio, Brittania Glass, in 1983. "This part of the valley system had a particular softness and it is very fertile for an old country."

The Yarra's life-richness takes many forms. In a country like Australia where land-use can change very quickly, there is a comfortable ebb-and-flow of continuity in the Valley. Once there were beef cattle; there are still. Dairy herds took over from vines in the 1920s; now they co-exist. A good example is the Yarra Valley Dairy herd that can be seen grazing from the Wine Bar restaurant at Yering Station.

With its combination of large and small-scale food production, the Yarra Valley is a major area for brussels sprouts, for orchards (particularly apples and stone fruit), and for berries. On each of the highways through the Valley there are berry farms—those grown around the small towns of Seville and Wandin on the Warburton highway are particularly prized. On a much smaller scale are those growers whose foods appear at farmers' markets, fairs, shows, and in local shops.

Gold and logging were once major industries, but they have been metamorphosed. These days, logs are likely to be used as vineyard posts for the wineries that attract even more people than gold once did. At last count, there were 55 wineries in the Yarra Valley, ranging from small family enterprises to those owned by major international and national companies. Their cellar doors are enormously valuable aspects of wine tourism.

This aerial view of ferns at Mount Donna Buang is from an elevated, 40-metre-long viewing platform, part of a boardwalk in the state forest that enables visitors to look over old-growth mountain ash trees and myrtle beeches that are up to 400 years old.

Pure-bred dingos are becoming rarer because of interbreeding with domestic dogs. This dingo lives with 200 other species of Australian wildlife that reside in the bushland at Healesville Sanctuary, an important arm of the Melbourne Zoo that opened in 1934.

first vineyard was in partnership with scientist Bailey Carrodus. The resulting wineries were Mount Mary, Seville Estate, Wantirna Estate and Yarra Yering. All but Seville Estate are still in family hands, and in second and even third generations.

It was a small but very lively scene in the 1960s, and all the early ventures are still in operation, although many have changed hands. Graham Miller (Chateau Yarinya, now De Bortoli), Peter Fergusson (Fergusson's) and Ernie Cester (St Hubert's) all planted vineyards then, while Darren and Farley Kelly started making cider at Kellybrook. And, for the first time since 1921, there were vines again at Yeringberg when Guill de Pury planted them in 1969.

So what caused the interest? Guill de Pury insists that wine-drinking had never disappeared in Melbourne. He remembers lunching as a boy with his father and wine merchants at the Florentino when wine was supplied as part of the meal, in a version of the "two courses and glass of wine" lunch specials that exist today.

The Florentino, like most good restaurants in Melbourne then, was owned by an Italian family, for whom wine was as much part of the table as food. The wine, however, was not always as good as the food. Peter McMahon remembers being given wine by an Italian patient who had a tiny vineyard that he had planted in the 1920s for his own use. The winery was primitive, the wines stored in blackened barrels and drawn off as wanted. Peter McMahon recalls it tasted like balsamic vinegar.

The first vignerons had been pastoralists or immigrant wine-makers. But when the renaissance began in the 1960s, it was driven by a happy co-incidence of doctors, lawyers and chemists—clever people with energy and a great enthusiasm for life. There were John Middleton and Peter McMahon, doctors with the Lilydale Medical practice, and Reg Egan, a lawyer, whose

The Italian Cester family, who were primarily poultry farmers, re-established St Hubert's commercially in 1966 (albeit in a different location from Hubert de Castella's original). Its early winemakers were three wine-interested men who worked together in brewing research at Carlton & United Breweries. Two of them, Alex White and Martin Grinbergs, went on to establish Lillydale Vineyards, while the third, David Lance, set up Diamond Valley with his wife Kathy.

There was much energy in the Yarra's renaissance, but there wasn't much to show for it until well into the 1980s. Alex White remembers that in 1986, when he, Martin and David made the wine for St Hubert's, Lillydale and Diamond Valley, the combined crush of about 625 tonnes represented approximately half the wine of the Yarra Valley. Compare that with 14,000 tonnes in 2001 for a snapshot of the growth since then! By far the largest producer of Melbourne's wine regions, the Yarra yields an annual total of around one million cases.

Its remarkable growth was paralleled in other parts of Australia. In the decades after those first tentative family vineyards in the mid-1960s, Australians metaphorically sharpened their knives and forks, waggled their chopsticks and polished their glasses. Australia became a wine-producing and wine-drinking nation, with an annual per capita consumption that is the highest in the English-speaking world. By the mid-1980s, Melburnians had become enthusiastic and discerning about what they ate and drank, and were keen to know more. They headed out to visit whatever cellar doors were open, they went to eat spit-roast beef at Fergusson's and at Yarra Burn, and sang along with Darren Kelly at Kellybrook. Meet-the-winemaker dinners became a feature of city restaurants.

Healesville was still a country town, recalls Dianne Clarke of Strathvea, a place where people stopped for a chat on the streets and where no one was in a hurry. At that time, the Healesville Hotel would have served more beer than wine with its counter meals. Now the wine list is a compendium of Yarra Valley and other wines, with an impressive list of French, Spanish and Italian wines that attracts all those who work in wineries and want to drink something new.

What is it that makes the Yarra Valley so special? Dr. Tony Jordan, chief executive and winemaker of Domaine Chandon, sums it up: "It's a bloody good valley."

His view is shared by a number of companies. Marcus Besen, one of Melbourne's most important businessmen, made a major investment in the future of the Yarra Valley for pinot noir and chardonnay when he established Tarrawarra in 1983. In the same year, Louis Bialkower, a partner in a major law firm, established Yarra Ridge, selling his fruit to another partner in the firm, James Halliday, one

The gardens at Strathvea near Healesville, are a great drawcard for birdlovers with their displaying peacocks and a wide range of Australian natives including rosellas, cockatoos, wattlebirds, currawongs and magpies. Strathvea is the last of the original 1920s guesthouses that attracted Melbournians away from the summer heat.

of Australia's most considerable wine identities (maker, judge and writer), who went on to set up Coldstream Hills.

Once the big wine companies—De Bortoli, BRL Hardy, McWilliam's and Southcorp—bought in, the importance of Yarra fruit was confirmed again and again through the 1980s and 90s. De Bortoli recognised the tourism potential of the winery: its restaurant and associated activities (cooking classes with guest chefs among them) now attract about 130,000 visitors annually. When the Rathbone family acquired Yering Station, they invested not only in wine, but also in tourism, building a complex that included an architecturally significant restaurant and winery, along with the re-fitted old barn, and the original winery as cellar door-cum-gallery.

When the champagne house of Moet & Chandon wanted to establish an Australian venture (a companion to those in Brazil, Argentina, California and later Spain), Dr Jordan, then an enological consultant, found the site for it in the Yarra Valley in 1987. The range of climates and soils within the Valley made it ideal for sparkling wine, and Domaine Chandon quickly became the leading super-premium Australian sparkling wine. It also became one of the focal tourism points of the Yarra.

"When you talk to Europeans, they roll their eyes when you tell them it's an area for pinot, chardonnay, cabernet and shiraz," says Dr Jordan. In European terms, that's like combining Bordeaux, Champagne, Burgundy, and the Rhone in one small area.

However, that's exactly what many makers do in the Yarra Valley. At Yering Station, the range includes sparkling (in a joint venture with

Champagne Devaux), the Bordeaux varieties (cabernet sauvignon, merlot, cabernet franc), pinot noir, chardonnay, shiraz, viognier, and marsanne. The latter has always grown well in the Yarra Valley—it was the grape known as "white hermitage" for which Yeringberg won international medals, trophies and prizes in the late-19th century.

At Lillydale Vineyards, near the small town of Seville, there is also gewurztraminer in the vineyards. This hard-to-pronounce Alsatian grape occupies a wonderful site there, along with riesling, chardonnay, sauvignon blanc, cabernet sauvignon, and merlot. When McWilliam's, one of Australia's big-ten companies, acquired the winery in the mid-1990s, no one was quite sure about the gewurztraminer. Max McWilliam, who took over the running of the place, determined the vines should stay and that the spice-and-lychee-scented dry wine should remain in the portfolio. It was a wise decision as it consistently wins gold medals in the show circuits—as do many Yarra wines.

Strawberry farms are a feature of the Yarra Valley, and in season, travellers can buy from roadside stalls. The Valley is also an important area for berries, cherries and other orchard fruit, as well as vegetables, mushrooms, and farmed salmon.

Yarra Valley reds are elegant, distinctive, and long-lived—should they have the chance to age. Case in point was a 1915 Yeringberg cabernet sauvignon that was found in a bricked-up cellar in Tasmania. In 1992 it was drunk in company that included English wine writer Hugh Johnson. The following day, when asked what was the best wine he had ever drunk, he replied: "the 1915!". In addition to this, James Halliday also named the wine as one of his top six.

The whites age well too. When an 1887 Yeringberg white hermitage was served as a masked wine at the Viticultural Society of Victoria in 1989, it drank beautifully, like a very fine 20-year-old French white burgundy.

So much is known about the early wines because the de Pury family records are wonderfully complete archives. Painted by Samuel de Pury, a portrait of Barak, the Aboriginal elder who died in 1903, still hangs in the family's living room. As does a reproduction of an affectionate drawing by Barak of Yeringberg that was sent to Samuel when he was in Europe. Guill's father's notebook contains a wealth of information including mention of the ration of wine that used to be given to the men

Autumn in the Yarra Valley. Pinot noir grapevines are recognisable in this season by their red leaves.

who worked on the de Pury property: "They could buy three bottles every Saturday evening. That used to keep them from going to the pub at Coldstream and getting drunk."

One of the relative newcomers to the Yarra Valley is Dominique Portet, who chose the area because he felt he understood cabernet—how it would grow, and how best to handle it. Portet, who has lived in Australia for nearly 30 years, comes from a long line of Bordeaux wine makers, and is the ninth-recorded generation of his family to be involved in wine—the line goes back further, but records were lost in the French Revolution. His brother Bernard is in the Napa in California at Clos du Val. For Dominique, the attraction of the Yarra Valley was the quality of its wines, especially the cabernet and merlot. "I found the fragrance, aromatics and structure —most of all the structure—reminds me of Bordeaux," he explains.

The cool climate is wonderful for pinot noir, one of the best in Australia. Its list of makers includes Coldstream Hills, Yering Station, Domaine Chandon, Tarrawarra, Gembrook Hills, Diamond Valley, De Bortoli, Yarra Ridge, St Hubert's, Wantirna Estate, Sticks, Long Gully, Yarra Burn, Bianchet, Mount Mary, Yeringberg —and that's not all. Each part of the Valley has its own flavour profile, just as each winery knows the special vineyards for pinot noir. In good years, reserve wines are made that pick up national and international awards. One of the nicest was the 1991 Tarrawarra pinot noir, which won Champion Red Wine in the Royal Melbourne Wine Show in 1993. Quite an accomplishment for a winery, as it is extremely difficult for a pinot to stand its ground against thousands of other, usually bigger wines.

Dr Jordan is a firm believer in the potential of shiraz in the Yarra Valley, and has enough confidence in the variety to have planted his own vineyard with it. Although the market has traditionally preferred the bigger, richer South Australian style, Dr Jordan thinks there will be a market for the spicy Rhone-style.

Like Napoleon's army, travellers march on their bellies. Melbourne's army of foodlovers is constantly on the move, seeking the newly delicious as well as old favourites. Suzanne Halliday, who is married to wine-identity James Halliday, learnt about the area and its strengths while living at Coldstream Hills. She was a driving force behind the formation of the Yarra Valley Regional Food Group, which now has more than 100 members. Beginning with the Aumann family orchards at Warrandyte, they form a food trail that includes farms, markets, restaurants, hotels, produce stores, herb farms and wineries. The Farmers' Market, held every month in the old barn at Yering Station, provides a snapshot of local produce and producers, from bakers to ice-cream makers and vegetable growers. Many Food Group members also have their own retail outlets.

In the spring and summer, there are local strawberry, raspberry, cherry and apple festivals. The area from Doncaster onwards used to be major apple orchard country, but suburban growth has swallowed those closest to Melbourne, although Petty's Orchard remains as a showcase and a museum for older varieties.

Fruit festivals sound old-fashioned cute, but fruit growing is still big business. Wild About

Fruit began in the 1930s with three hectares of apples. Now, in its third generation, the company grows more than 20 varieties of cherries and 13 varieties of apples. Its orchards cover up to 160 hectares in the Yarra Valley (and over 800 hectares elsewhere), and the company has developed a sophisticated range

Richard Shenfield, viticulturalist at Coldstream Hills, inspects the grapes at vintage time. Viticulturalists are responsible for the maintenance and health of the vineyards, from pruning to picking.

of fruit juices and vinegar, in addition to the fruit that goes to Melbourne and other markets. They're not the only company to boast longevity: most orchardists here are into their third generation.

Nothing happens in Melbourne without food. The biggest festival event in the Yarra Valley is Grape Grazing, an annual weekend in February when restaurants team up with wineries and offer entrée-sized helpings of food matched with a glass of wine. There's usually music at each winery as well, and the event attracts thousands of participants.

In the Yarra, the best local restaurants and cafés pride themselves on serving locally grown food. Some city restaurants are equally fervent supporters, their menus noting Yarra Valley-grown food (berries, stone fruit, apples, cheese, salmon and salmon roe) and wine. St Kilda restaurateur Ronnie Di Stasio has house wines that are a cut above the usual—pinot noir and chardonnay from his own Yarra Valley vineyards.

There's music in them there hills, too. What many wine companies have found is that people who like music like food and wine as well. As a result, musical programmes are calendar fixtures at Tarrawarra, Domaine Chandon, Eyton on Yarra, and Yering Station. The most remarkable is the Sun Microsystems weekend at Domaine Chandon—a solid weekend of chamber music recitals in the Riddling Hall, punctuated by meals.

Because the Yarra Valley is only an hour out of town, it seems scarcely worth staying the night. But that's changing now, reverting to the fashion of earlier days when Melburnians headed into the hills for rest and recreation.

Until recently, accommodation was mostly limited to motels and bed-and-breakfast establishments. Chateau Yering established a market for serious luxury (following the demise of Burnham Beeches), and then the Yarra Valley acquired its first major hotel, the 102-room Sebel Lodge, complete with conference facilities, and a Jack Nicklaus designed golf course. It's an up-to-date version of the old Warburton Chalet, which in its day was one of the biggest guesthouses in Victoria.

It is unlikely that the Yarra Valley will be over-run by big hotel groups. The strategy of the Yarra Ranges Shire is to limit development, which means that residential housing will not be making major claims on vineyard land or operations. In shires closer to Melbourne, there are difficulties because local residents take the view that agriculture and horticulture are nice to look at, but have no place next door.

Wine is the way into the Yarra Valley, but the enduring richness of the area is that there is still be more than enough to do for those who wouldn't know a cabbage from a chardonnay. The wide stillness of the Valley makes it a great area for ballooning. The river system means there is good fishing and even canoeing. The forests make it an extremely rewarding environment for bushwalking and bird watching. The regional food group ensures everyone knows how to track down the pleasures of berrying and cheese-tasting. The network of towns—Warburton, Healesville, Yarra Glen and Warrandyte—provide galleries to admire and buy local arts and crafts. In short, as Hubert de Castella put it, the valley provides "a succession of most romantic landscapes".

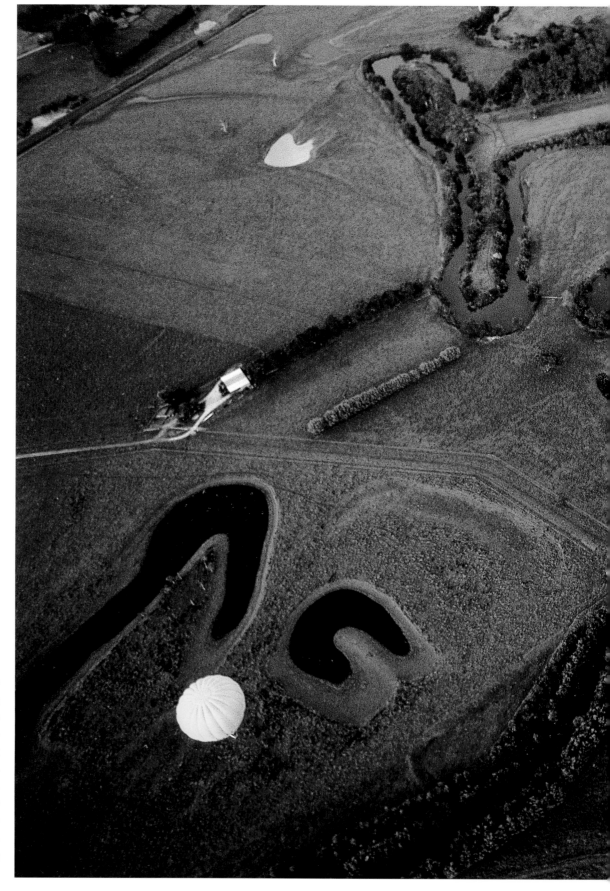

Ballooning is the perfect way to enjoy the scenery along the Yarra River, and its surrounding 4,000-square-kilometre rural catchment area. Rising in the mountains to the east of Warburton, the river takes the long way to the sea, creating many loops and ox-bow lakes in its 245-kilometre course, until it finally enters Port Phillip Bay.

In the golden morning light *(left)*, the extent of the Yarra Valley reveals itself—hills and forests, farmland, dams and vineyards. Soft clouds *(above)* are a feature of the landscape. Close to the ground, they make welcome mist and fog that protect the vines from frost.

The favoured sites in the Yarra Valley are on slopes facing north or north-east. Good wine doesn't just happen: it starts in the vineyard, where there is always work to be done *(right)*, such as the annual spring programme to control powdery and downy mildew.

The rows of vines are dressed in their autumn best at Oakridge Estate *(above)* and Coldstream Hills *(right)*. Visitors sometimes think nets impede the view of the vines, but for vignerons, netting is an important part of vineyard management. The nets keep out the birds that would otherwise destroy the crop. They are usually draped over two or three rows of vines and are removed just before the grapes are picked.

As vintage time starts, work patterns change. At Yeringberg *(above)*, the mechanical harvester moves in to pick grapes before they are crushed. At Gembrook Hills *(left)*, the cleaning starts: Ian Marks and winemaker Timo Mayer are washing out barrels before filling them with red wine. The white tank in the background will be used to ferment their sauvignon blanc.

The shiraz is being crushed at Seville Estate *(above)*, one of the first vineyards to start up in the Yarra Valley revival of the 1960s. John Middleton *(right)* a trailblazing figure with boundless energy and enthusiasm, established Mount Mary in 1972. The reputation of Mount Mary wines gave the Yarra Valley national and international recognition.

Yarra Valley families: David de Pury *(left)*, the fourth generation, checks the aromas on a newly pressed wine. At Wantirna Estate *(above)*, there are three generations: Reg Egan, winemaker daughter Maryann, and the grand-daughters who help with picking, and give their names to wines. Reg's wife Tina says that there are people who greet Isabella (beside her aunt Maryann) with surprise: "You're Isabella Chardonnay!".

The Yering Station Wine Bar restaurant *(previous page)* was designed to open the building to the landscape, quite unlike the earlier architecture of neighbouring luxury hotel Chateau Yering *(above)*. The two were once one property, settled first by the Ryrie brothers in 1838, then by Paul de Castella, who built the homestead that has been turned into the hotel. The tasting room at Domaine Chandon *(right)* is a showcase site for the Yarra Valley.

Peter Fergusson *(above)* was one of the first to see the tourism potential for the Yarra Valley. The restaurant he established alongside his winery in the 1970s is famous for its spit-roasts. James Halliday *(right)* is one of Australia's foremost wine writers and founder of Coldstream Hills. His wife Suzanne has been an enthusiastic and hardworking supporter of the broad range of Yarra Valley produce, and is at the forefront of the Yarra Valley Regional Food Group.

The Lilydale Agricultural Show is a great meeting place and provides a chance to observe and participate in displays of rural skills. A mother *(above left)*, checks the precision of her daughter's Scottish dancing footwork while a shearer *(above right)*, shows off his skills. Whatever the age *(opposite)*, there is always room for hot dogs and chips.

Artists from north and south of the Yarra Valley: potter David Williams *(left)* at Toolangi has perfected highly prized crystalline glazes on classic forms. The blues and greens of the finished pots reflect the colours of the landscape. Rob Knottenbelt *(above)* is a glass artist working from his studio at Brittania Creek. His glass sculptures are in galleries in Dusseldorf and New York, as well as national collections.

The peacefulness of the Yarra Valley often makes it seem much further away from Melbourne than a good hour's drive. There's plenty of room to move alongside the Melba Highway, where paddocks, vineyards and bushland co-exist. East of Healesville *(above)* is the Maroondah Reservoir Park, one of the most popular parks in Victoria, which includes gardens, wildlife, and walking trails that go through forests of native and exotic trees.

The Yarra Ranges National Park, declared in 1995, extends from Healesville to Warburton, and takes in streams, creeks and luxuriant rainforest. In the 1850s, the Yarra River at Warburton *(above and opposite)* was busy with goldminers seeking their fortune. Now Warburton combines fishing, picnicking, history and old hippy enclaves. Overleaf: Early morning mist veils the Yarra Valley, described by Hubert de Castella, a 19th-century, Swiss-born vigneron as "a succession of most romantic landscapes."

CHAPTER THREE

MORNINGTON PENINSULA

The Mornington Peninsula is a relatively small area but it packs in an enormous amount. For this curl of land, which separates Port Phillip Bay from Western Port and Bass Strait, is Melbourne's playground, everyone's day trip, everyone's summer holiday. This is Melbourne's day out and beach house.

It is an unusually fruitful playground, with farms, orchards, chickens, market gardens and vineyards, along with golf courses, racecourses, art galleries, plant nurseries and surf and bay beaches. It may be a single area, but it has myriad smaller ones that are defined by its geography. There is always a play of opposites throughout the Peninsula: mountains and gullies, ridges and flats, cosy smooth beaches and wild surf; dense coastal housing and rural farmland, professional fishing and recreational yachting, multi-million-dollar houses and summer camping grounds. The interplay between the glamorous and daggy is what gives the Peninsula such a buzz.

One of the best introductions to the area is the Red Hill Market, which is held on the first Sunday of the month from September to May. Red Hill is the richest part of the Peninsula in terms of food and wine, and the market attracts huge crowds. The car park and the roadside are a clutter of battered old utilities, trucks and luxury cars, and the market is a flourishing tangle of locally grown fruit, vegetables, flowers and plants, home-made preserves, biscuits, juices, snack food, and crafts and musicians.

The entry point to the Mornington Peninsula has changed over time. These days most people come from Melbourne, and the general view is that the Peninsula starts at Oliver's Hill, beyond Frankston. The first European settlements came from the opposite direction, since they accessed the Peninsula by sea, coming through the Heads, the surprisingly narrow entrance to Port Phillip Bay. There's a marker for the first European settlement—a convict camp in 1803—at Sorrento. After the long, difficult voyage from England, they must have sailed through the Heads, and fallen thankfully onto the welcoming strand. That's still how Sorrento feels—a smooth and beautiful beach.

Each beach, each hill and each town has its own identity. Sorrento is a couple of kilometres from Portsea, and quite different. So is Blairgowrie, Rye and all the other beach towns. Merricks, Shoreham and Flinders, on the eastern side of the Peninsula, are quite different from Mount Martha, Rosebud and Dromana.

The Mornington Peninsula provides sheltered beaches on the Port Phillip Bay side, and wilder surf beaches on the ocean side, where the chill waters of Bass Strait are to be taken seriously. It was at this beach at Portsea *(left)*, that Prime Minister Harold Holt disappeared, presumed drowned, in the summer of 1967.

A quick guide for beginners: Portsea is where the seriously big money from Melbourne goes, Dromana is everyone's holiday ground, Mount Eliza is largely residential, Mount Martha's holiday houses have always attracted Melbourne professionals (including Yarra Valley winemakers), and there are never any summer hordes disturbing the peace at Shoreham or Flinders.

At Safety Beach, near Mount Martha, a monument erected by the local foreshore committee tells a fascinating tale. Safety Beach was one of the area's first gazetted names, thanks to the efforts of John Aitken in 1836. He was moving his livestock from Tasmania aboard the brig *Chili*, but ran aground and ended up rowing half his sheep ashore, landing them safely on that beach.

In the early days of European settlement, the Mornington Peninsula was farming land before it became holiday territory. Nineteenth-century pastoral Australia needed land constantly for its sheep and cattle, and this region proved suitable, especially since it was close to Melbourne. The ever-growing city needed food, and the Peninsula provided apples and other fruit, as well as meat and fish. Land was cleared, and land was drained —especially on the eastern seaward side of the Peninsula. From early on, Melburnians liked to holiday by the seaside. It's hard to imagine now

Beach boxes, originally changing sheds, now provide bright beach-side storage for locals. Here at Mornington Beach *(below)* they make a colourful backdrop for drinks on the sand.

what it was like when the indigenous Bunurong people lived here, when there were no houses. But the lie of the land, with its distinctive landmark hills (Oliver's Hill, Mount Eliza, Mount Martha and Arthur's Seat) is unmistakable.

The visitor can read the history even from the road. The huge cypress pines that border the roadsides are a legacy of earlier farming. There are still great old houses that were built by prosperous families: the McCrae homestead, Heronswood, The Briars, and the old Grimwade house at Coolart. The coolstores that once kept apples now house art galleries, regional stores and wineries. The brightly coloured huts on the beach have their own stories: built in grander times, then neglected, they have now been restored in bright colours, bold indicators of their rising value.

The Mornington Peninsula is unusual among Melbourne's wine regions because it is a relatively new vineyard area. There had been vines planted on the Peninsula (The Briars provides a record of that), but the wines were never a match for those of the Yarra, Geelong, or Sunbury.

Vineyard growth has accelerated with the speed of the Porsches that roar along the freeways to Portsea. Thirty years ago there were no wineries in the region—now there are more than 50, and that figure doesn't include the vineyards on Phillip and French Islands, clearly visible from the eastern side of the Peninsula. French Island, named for the French explorer Nicolas Baudin, used to be a prison farm. Now it is an eco-tour island with an organic farm and restaurant, as well as vineyards.

Among the Peninsula's wine pioneers were Nat and Rosalie White, who planted their first

vines in the mid-1970s at Main Ridge. Main Ridge is not a promising site for fine wine. It has high rainfall, and a cool climate. But the Whites have succeeded in maintaining what the Peninsula does really well. They produce very limited quantities of high quality wine whose flavours clearly reflect the nature of the site.

Castle-like Delgany at Portsea was built as a private residence in the 1920s, and later served as a hospital and school before being renovated and turned into a luxury hotel.

The Whites had become interested in regional wines when they lived in Europe, and they planted chardonnay and pinot noir because they thought the climate was rather like that of Burgundy. Their production is sold mainly by mail order or cellar-door sales, which is the way of many here.

The Peninsula's climates (there's more than one) make for distinctive wines. With its maritime influences—no extremes of temperature, prevailing winds, and a cool, usually reliable autumn—the long slow ripening season gives intense flavours to its grapes and wines. Mornington Peninsula's pinot noir often shows plum and spice characters; chardonnay can be richly complex; shiraz in a warm year has lively pepper and spice notes; while sauvignon blanc is rounder and fuller than its Marlborough counterpart. In a good year, the cabernet shows up well, too, especially at the northern end. In a good year. That's the catch phrase here. In less good years, the wines are still fine, but unlikely to age for more than a few years. In awful years (cool weather and wind in spring, wet summer and autumn), crops can be so diminished it is a toss-up whether it is worth picking the grapes at all.

Overall production, it should be noted, is small. In total, the Mornington Peninsula produces only about a tenth of the Yarra Valley's production from nearly as many wineries. By and large, this is boutique winery country. There are some places that open only twice a year (for the Queen's Birthday and Melbourne Cup Weekend festivals). Others open once a month, usually on the first Sunday. Others are

open at weekends, or by appointment. And still others provide a winery with the lot: cellar door, restaurant, and even accommodation and conference facilities.

For a small area, there's a remarkable biodiversity of wines, flavours, and business styles. To a large extent, it has been driven by people who've established their professional

lives in other fields—specialist doctors, high-profile lawyers, teachers and publishers. For some, the establishment of a vineyard was a kind of toe-in-the-water. The scenario goes something like this: "I/we are interested in wine, we live/would like to live part-time/full-time on the Peninsula, and it would be great to have a vineyard and make our own wine. If it works out,

we can move to a new career." The successful ones include Moorooduc Estate, Paringa Estate, and Turramurra. Often it doesn't work out so well, because vineyards on the Peninsula need careful and costly management, and some years are disasters because of poor weather.

Never mind the bad years. This is daydream country. Call in at Dromana Estate, order a

The autumn view from the cellar door at Tuck's Ridge is one of many that brings on a daydream attack: Why don't we sell the house in Melbourne? Why don't we plant a vineyard like this?

Alex White *(below)* checks out the flavours of the grapes before the crush. His winemaking started in the Yarra Valley; now he works mainly on the Mornington Peninsula, where his range extends to Italian (including dolcetto and arneis) and Spanish varieties.

glass or a bottle and a plate of food. Sit on the balcony admiring the lake, the trees, the vines, the ducks, the crowds. It takes a heart of stone not to be tempted to throw everything in and plant a vineyard with a little weekend restaurant. Stonier's has the same effect. The view from the cellar door at Tuck's Ridge makes people dreamy and thoughtful. The big players do it best, but every place with a view brings

out an attack of "what if". What makes it so tempting is that pretty well everywhere has a view. There's the broad sweep of the Bay from The Peak restaurant at Arthurs Seat, there's the hillside vines and olive grove at Montalto, the secluded vineyard from Mantons Creek, the winery and vines at La Baracca at T'Gallant, and the gardens and vines at Moorooduc Estate.

At the southern end of the Peninsula, there is another attraction again. Artist John Dent, who lives in Sorrento, observes that it is particularly good country for family holidays. There are gentle bay beaches for smaller children, and Gunnamatta's surf beach for teenagers. Lots for the kids to do, and there's also golf at Portsea and at Cape Schanck, the wild southern-most point. There's sailing too, all along the Bay coast.

The Mornington Peninsula is a kind of terrier among wine regions, snapping at the heels of the bigger ones. Because vineyards are often small, and high-cost viticulture has forced owners to think about what might sell (if we can't compete on price, how are we going to compete?), this has always been the area to find something new. When the Whites first planted their chardonnay and pinot noir, closely followed by the Keffords at Merricks Estate, they were new varieties. Garry Crittenden at Dromana Estate has been a champion of a range of Italian varieties— dolcetto, barbera, arneis and pinot grigio. At T'Gallant, Kath Quealy and her husband Kevin have been tireless promoters of pinot grigio (known in French as pinot gris). Every grape gets a go on the Mornington Peninsula: there's pinot meuniere, gewurztraminer, even the Spanish red variety tempranillo.

Everything grows well here, including roses, whose decorative presence at the end of vineyard rows has given rise to all kinds of horticultural furphies. They are not an early-warning system for vine disease (although they are susceptible to some of the same problems), and anyone who relied on roses as an indicator would be in dire trouble.

With its endless days of wine and roses, along with great produce like fruit, vegetables, cultivated mussels, seafood, chickens and eggs, there should be great restaurants, especially since everyone is interested in regional food. However, eating well on the Peninsula has traditionally been difficult, with just a couple of professionally run bright spots. The tourist season only runs from Christmas until the end of January, when the Peninsula population multiplies alarmingly. A six-week season is not enough to make a viable business, and even the weekend restaurant is a challenge in terms of staff and ongoing business. It can be done successfully, but it's harder than in Melbourne.

The future for eating well is looking decidedly brighter, largely because of the increasing number of wineries. Summer holidays or not, there are lots of good reasons to visit the area. Wineries attract a growing number of visitors who come because they enjoy wine and food. A winery restaurant enables them to see the wine in a more relaxed environment than a tasting room, and they are likely to buy more wine ("What a fabulous experience, we'll take half a dozen") and then return because they know there's something good to eat and so much else to do. One day there will be lunch at Montalto, the next at Willow Creek, the

following lunch at Red Hill Estate, or perhaps a wine dinner at Poff's one weekend, or at The Peak. As well, for gardening gourmets, there's the café at Heronswood that features house-grown produce.

The trend used to be do-it-yourself: holiday houses or camping grounds, with only a few motels and some bed-and-breakfast places. As working patterns have changed—shorter breaks for

Surgeon-winemaker Richard McIntyre and his wife Jill established Moorooduc Estate at the warmer northern end of the Peninsula. Their wines—especially the wild yeast pinot noir and chardonnay—have attained a considerable name, and their property now extends to a restaurant and accommodation.

busier professionals, and more conferences—so have the options. The restoration of Delgany at Portsea, an inventive castle-like building of local stone, to a country house hotel, was the beginning. Delgany had been built on "the most beautiful spot on the most favoured peninsula" (as *Home Beautiful* magazine gushingly put it in the late 1920s) by Harold Armytage, whose family lived at Como in Melbourne. Lindenderry, at Red Hill, is another country house hotel with generous rooms, conference facilities, gardens, a restaurant, a vineyard and an impressive art collection.

There are two regional art galleries on the Peninsula—at Mornington, and at Langwarrin—as well as lots of private galleries. The first director of the Mornington Peninsula Regional Art Gallery was art writer Alan McCulloch. Its focus is on the artists of the area, with a collection that includes some wonderful Boyd family paintings. Arthur Boyd lived with his grandparents, Arthur and Minnie Boyd, at Rosebud for three happy years when he was a teenager. The Mornington gallery has developed an arts trail so visitors can collect a map and drive to selected places of painterly significance. The McClelland Gallery at Langwarrin, situated in a bushland sculpture park, is also on the trail. The trail is a rich one, since so many painters have lived or painted here, including Georgiana McCrae, Louis Buvelot, Penleigh Boyd, Arthur Boyd, Albert Tucker, Fred Williams and Rick Amor.

The all-you-could-wish-for nature of the Peninsula may well threaten the profusion of its wines. Vineyards are limited by more than geography. As more people choose to live on the Peninsula, there have been more objections to the presence of vineyards and wineries. Those who have spent a million or so to live in the tranquillity of the Peninsula often object to the presence of noisy agricultural activity, especially winemaking. Expensive legal challenges, increasing land costs, and a gambler's climate will likely mean that the future will be in managing the region's enviable resources, rather than extending them.

When Nat and Rosalie White planted pinot noir and chardonnay at Main Ridge Estate *(left)* in the 1970s, they purposely kept yields low to maximize quality. During vintage time, family and friends pitch in to help harvest the grapes and are rewarded with fine food and wine.

Artist John Dent *(left)* has painted landscapes throughout Australia, but lives in Sorrento, where he says the lifestyle enables people to achieve their dreams. Lunch at Montalto *(above)* is part of the dream achieved by owner John Mitchell, who has planted olives and vines on the property. The restaurant's first chef was Philippe Mouchel, whose classic French training and devotion to regional food added greatly to the distinction of the Peninsula.

The Mornington Peninsula is a cool climate in Australian terms, but its proximity to the sea means there are never frosts. Vineyards are planted on slopes that catch the sun, and the long ripening season gives distinctively intense flavours to the wines.

Artists Janet and Mike Green *(left)* both have their studios in their Mount Eliza home, and have watched the area change from farmland to residential. Their own work has made important transitions in the decades they have lived in their area. Janet's work combines still life with landscape. Mike's references are personal, historical and sculptural. Clive Blazey *(above)* and his wife Penny run the historic property of Heronswood, which is now one of the most important garden resources in Victoria. Its café features Heronswood-grown produce, much of which comes from heritage varieties.

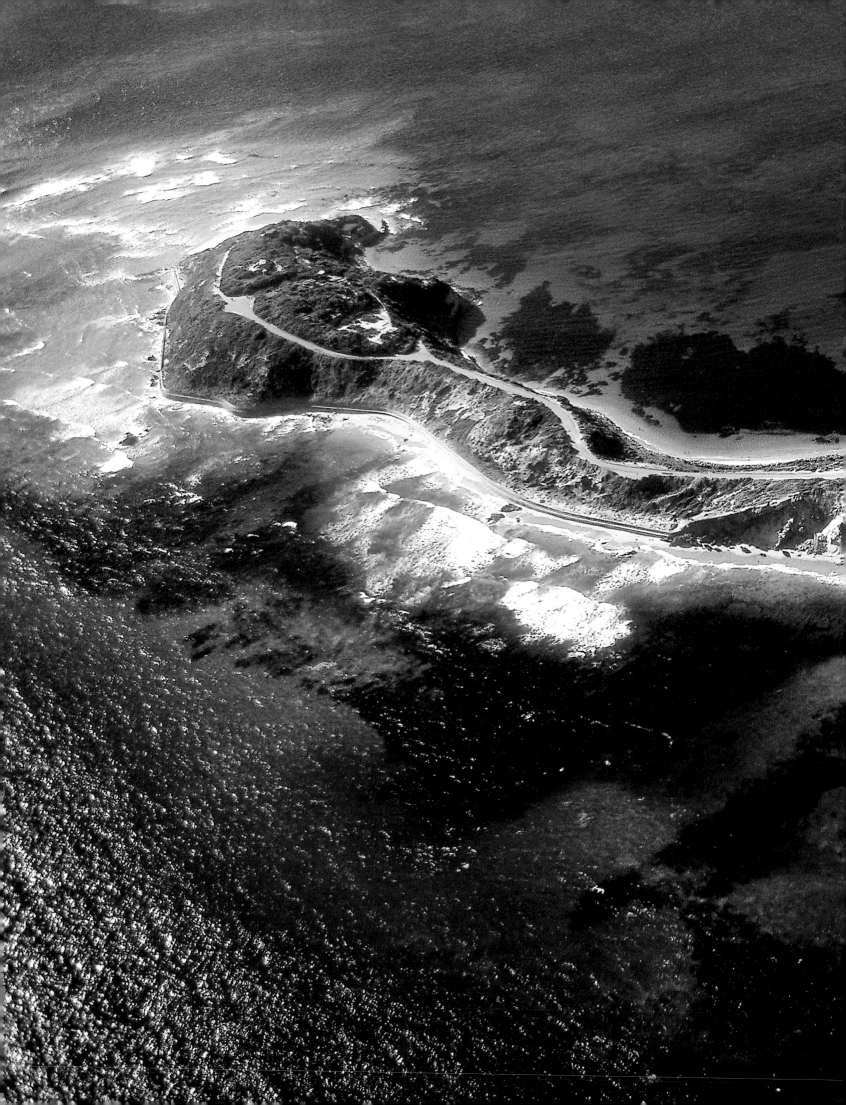

Previous pages: Point Nepean, the westernmost point of the Mornington Peninsula, is classified by the National Trust for its landscape, and by the Australian Heritage Commission for its history. From the 19th to the mid-20th century it was a quarantine station and military base. Red Hill Estate *(above)* looks out on Western Port Bay. At Blairgowrie *(right)*, the sea is at its most recreational.

A boardwalk *(left)* leads safely across Cape Schanck, the southernmost point of the Mornington Peninsula, where the waters of Bass Strait are often wild. Some of the beach boxes at Mornington *(above)* were once derelict and there was discussion about removing them. These days they are occasions for artful pride.

The Mornington Peninsula is farm land still. The market gardens around Boneo *(above)* provide food for Melbourne. There are roadside stalls from which to buy tomatoes and other vegetables, fruit, and eggs. At Ellisfield at Red Hill *(right)*, Melburnians and locals come to pick the many varieties of cherries, as well as quinces. Ellisfield garlic is also highly prized.

Vineyards on the Mornington Peninsula range from boutique-small to larger scale enterprises *(above)*. Mount Martha *(right)* is one of the distinctive hills of the Peninsula. Its best known feature is the long beach which was the attraction for early holiday makers. The newer housing developments are sited for views, not proximity to beach. Safety Beach, so called because it was where an early European settler rowed his sheep safely to shore, is just around the headland.

Sorrento was the site of the first European settlement in Victoria. The ferries from the city arriving at Sorrento and then at Portsea were important transport for early residents and holiday makers. Today the much-loved pier at Portsea attracts fishermen hoping to catch whiting, flathead or snapper for dinner.

CHAPTER FOUR

GEELONG

Geelong, Victoria's second-largest city, is only 80 kilometres southwest of Melbourne. At the hub of a wheel, it is the centre of its own circle of pleasure. It is a gateway city: the way to Melbourne from the west, the way to the surf beaches and seaside towns of the Bellarine Peninsula, or onwards to the Great Ocean Road, or the Western District.

Once Geelong nearly rivalled Melbourne as Victoria's main port. The city was admirably situated as a transport centre for the great loads of wheat, wool and hides that came there from the fertile Western District, especially when the railway linked up Ballarat and Geelong. The importance of 19th- century Geelong can still be seen in all its public buildings, in the immense bluestone warehouses, the grandeur of the railway station, and the Geelong Art Gallery, with its splendid collection.

Once, too, Geelong rivalled the Yarra Valley for sheer numbers of vineyards. By Ebenezer Ward's 1863 account, there were vineyards everywhere, starting with Neuchatel, that was first planted in 1842. The early Swiss settled here with alacrity: the Messieurs Brequet, Amiet, Dunoyer, Chollet, Dardel (who was brought to the Yarra Valley to make wine at Yering Station in

the early days), Belperroud and Pettavel. As well, there were the non-Swiss—Dr Hope and Misters Creed, Hall and Mathews, and all those German colonists at Germantown, six kilometres from Geelong on the way to Apollo Bay.

Artist Jan Mitchell's colourful bollards tell Geelong's story in another way. Her painted totem-like figures that stand like cheerful sentinels along the Eastern shore and through the surrounding landscape are as much about the present as the past. They illustrate the region's history, but there is no soft-centred nostalgia to these bright and bold sculptures.

From Melbourne, Geelong is a straight but unlovely run along the Princes Highway. Halfway there is a turn-off to Werribee where Melbourne's water treatment plants are sited, providing an unexpected wetland for birds. With its flat land, rich soil, and easy access to Melbourne, Werribee is home to many market gardens. The best artichokes in Melbourne are grown here, along with broccoli, cauliflower, fennel, and a range of other greens.

This region's distinguished past and revitalised present are evident at Werribee Mansion, one of those splendid 19th-century towered mansions that abound in Melbourne's

Cunningham Pier is a legacy of Geelong's early major importance as a wool and wheat port, and was also known as Railway Pier. It has been redeveloped with shops and restaurants, and is still a popular fishing spot with locals.

surrounds. This once grand private house is now part of a tourism complex. There has been some fine architectural recycling: an adjoining former seminary is now a luxury hotel, with its immense gardens providing the autumn setting for the Helen Lempriere Sculpture Award, Melbourne's richest sculpture prize. The Shadowfax vineyards and strikingly modern winery and cellar door are right next door.

The rose-loving, horse-riding, safari-keen, wine-appreciative gourmet need proceed no further. This multi-faceted complex also plays host to Victoria's equestrian centre (polo championships in November), the State's rose gardens, and even an open-air zoo, where giraffe, rhinoceros and zebra wander near bison and antelope. The other imperative on the Geelong road is the You Yangs, the distinctive mountain range, so celebrated in the paintings of Fred Williams.

Geelong can also be reached from the south, from the Bellarine Peninsula which juts into Port Phillip Bay like its northern neighbour, the Mornington Peninsula. From the north, the bony land-finger of Portsea points straight at Point Lonsdale in the south, with only The Rip (Port Phillip Bay's entrance) to separate them. Queenscliff is tucked inside the Rip, its fortress still guarding against phantom World War I enemy fleets. At that time, it was feared the Russians were coming. They never did. The thing to watch out for these days are the dolphins that often accompany the ferries running to Sorrento and Portsea.

The Bellarine Peninsula is full of seaside towns. Queenscliff is the historic one, Torquay is the surfing one, and Point Lonsdale is renowned for family summer holidays because of its long, shallow, sandy beach. There's Barwon Heads and Ocean Grove, all looking sprucely residential, and peaceful Portarlington. Everyone, it seems, wants to live by the seaside these days

Once upon a time, everyone wanted to cultivate a vineyard in the Geelong area. The area's hopes went up in smoke when the appearance of phylloxera in 1877 caused so many vines to be grubbed out and burnt. Not all vines, however, were infected, and not all the vineyards were burnt. For the vineyard workers who might have stayed, there was better and easier money to be made on the goldfields, or in Melbourne. For nearly a century, there was nothing to suggest that Geelong had once been a major wine area.

The revival began in the 1960s, as it did in many areas throughout Australia. Here, the pioneer was a local veterinarian, Daryl Sefton, who had a considerable interest in wine. His great-grandparents, Regina and Jacob Just, had been among the Swiss immigrants who farmed the land from the 1840s onwards. They had

The ferry crossing from Sorrento to Queenscliff can sometimes reward observant passengers with glimpses of seals and dolphins in Port Phillip Bay. Because of the sheltered waters here, the crossing is usually quite smooth.

established the Pension Suisse in Geelong, which was a meeting place and a kind of wine bar for the Swiss of the area. Nini, Daryl's wife, says that he woke up one morning and made a decision: "I know what I want to do with the rest of my life. I want to revive the wine industry in Geelong."

The Seftons planted cabernet sauvignon, shiraz and gewurztraminer at their Idyll vineyard in Moorabool in the late 1960s, and were closely followed by Tom Maltby at Anakie Vineyard. Both released their first wines in 1971, marking an important beginning. A decade later, the vineyard that made Geelong known all over Australia was Bannockburn, whose winemaker Gary Farr opened everyone's palate to the possibilities of the area with his rich Burgundian-styled pinot noir and chardonnay. Bannockburn was never open to the public, and Gary Farr himself does not like to be a public figure. The wines, however, speak for themselves, and have a lot to say about Geelong and their maker. There is now another label—By Farr. And true to form, there's no cellar door for that, either.

Wine tourism is less strong in the Geelong area than Melbourne's other wine regions. That's not surprising, since there are only 16 wineries. For the most part, these are small enterprises, often on the sites of former vineyards. The wineries are now mostly situated around Anakie and Waurn Ponds, but there are others further afield on the Bellarine Peninsula, such as Will Wolseley near Torquay, and Scotchman's Hill at Drysdale.

Today's range of grape varieties is more limited than it was in the 1860s, when the

riotous viticultural mix included La Gloire, Black Hamburg, Chasselas, Dolcetto, Aucarot, and Carignan—to name but a few. But the range is still broad.

Paul Chambers, who owns Staughton Vale Vineyard and is a champion of regional vineyards (he presides over a number of industry organisations), points out that one of the unique features of the area is that there are sites

The pier at Point Lonsdale extends out into Port Phillip Bay where the calm bay waters meet the Bass Strait. The Rip, as it is known, is one of the most dangerous stretches of water on the Australian coastline.

capable of ripening a wide range of cultivars. His vineyard is a case in point. He's a Bordeaux fan, so he grows cabernet sauvignon and cabernet franc along with malbec and petit verdot, as well as riesling, semillon and chardonnay. Shiraz grows well around here, too. "As long as you've got the right site," he stresses.

Pinot noir does well in the Geelong area, producing wines of beautiful complexity. At Prince Albert vineyards, owner and winemaker Bruce Hyett planted only pinot noir in 1976. It was the first vineyard in Australia to be given over to that single variety, and was a bold statement of faith.

There are a couple of major ventures, such as Pettavel at Waurn Ponds, which is named for one of the first Swiss winemakers. At Drysdale, Scotchmans Hill (named for some of the non-Swiss early settlers) is owned by the same family that has transformed nearby Spray Farm. The old homestead, originally built in 1851, has been turned into a cellar door with a restaurant and courtyard, with formal gardens and a vineyard. Spray Farm's grounds are the setting for an international equestrian event in early December, and a summer music festival that attracts thousands to the big hill that looks out on the Bay, and the skyscrapers of Melbourne. Happily for the vines and summer crowds, the slopes are sheltered from the winds. By a quirk of nature, the sea breezes never seem to travel uphill.

The climate is drier here than on the other side of the Bay, the landscape less obviously pretty. What the Bellarine lacks in green, though, it makes up in blue—the blue of Port Phillip Bay and of the ocean. The water tugs at people in different ways: it's there for swimming, for fishing, for admiring, and most powerfully, for surfing.

"We're blessed we've got so many quality reef breaks between Torquay and Bell's Beach," says Darren Dickson, who has been surfing here for more than 20 years. He is equally blessed in his work. Attached to one of the seven companies making surfboards at Torquay, every time Darren goes out on one of his boards, he can say—honestly—that he's not only doing research and development, but also sales and marketing. He says there are always people who want to know how he can catch so many waves, and once they talk to him and try out one of his boards, he's made a sale.

Close to Torquay is Bell's Beach, home of the renowned Easter Classic, that has lured surfers from all over the world since 1963. Torquay's surfing museum tells the whole story of the sport's history with a hall of fame that includes international champion Wayne Lynch (who lives nearby), and Gail Couper, ten-times winner of the competition. Surfing is big business, with the Geelong/Torquay area employing more people than any other surf area in Australia. The biggest business is clothing: the famous brands of Rip Curl and Quiksilver began right here in 1969.

The Heritage town of Queenscliff, nestled near the entrance to the Bay, was a seaside resort from the 1880s and onwards. The old hotels that accommodated Victorian ladies and gentlemen are still there: the Queenscliff, Royal, Vue Grande and Ozone are all now grandly refurbished. The Queenscliff Hotel was the first, restored by the O'Donnell sisters with great feeling for the way it would have been, complete with working fireplaces in the bedrooms (but no en-suite bathrooms), a formal dining room, and sitting rooms. Its revival was followed by other restaurants and cafés, galleries, hotels, and bed-and-breakfast places, all of which are packed during the November music festival.

In 1983 the forest at Angahook State Park was reduced to a grey ash moonscape by the awful fires of Ash Wednesday, fires so intense that whole houses melted, leaving only chimneys and glass pebbles that had once been windows. The houses have been rebuilt along the Great Ocean Road that leads to Lorne and Apollo Bay, and the famous rock formations of the Twelve Apostles. It's wonderful strong country with a coastline that is a constant source of delight. But there is one catch. Wine-lovers be warned— there are no more vineyards until the far southwest of Victoria.

The complex at Werribee includes the National Equestrian Centre, the Victoria State Rose Garden, Werribee Park Mansion and Shadowfax winery. Polo is one of the attractions in November.

From the air *(above)*, the expanse of Bass Strait that meets the southern coast of the Bellarine Peninsula appears endless. The bridge that connects Barwon Heads and Ocean Grove is always busy during the summer, and is a popular fishing spot for nearby caravanners. From the slopes of Spray Farm at Drysdale *(right)*, on the northern side of the Bellarine Peninsula, the tall buildings of Melbourne are distinctly visible across the bay.

An aerial view of Scotchman's Hill vineyards *(above)* shows the extent of the vineyards established by David and Vivienne Browne. From the winery *(right)*, the largest in the area, comes wine under the Scotchman's Hill and Swan Bay labels. Pinot noir and sauvignon blanc do especially well in these sites.

Will Wolseley *(above)* is luckier than most when it comes to labelling the wines he makes from his vineyards near Torquay. The labels are designed by his father, artist John Wolseley, whose paintings of the Australian landscape are so sought after. Gary Farr *(right)* has been a great promoter of the Geelong area through his premium wines. The quality of his Burgundian-style pinot noir and chardonnay are recognised internationally.

Spring is festival time throughout Victoria. The Spring Harvest at Werribee *(left)* coincides with the polo and brings together a range of Victorian food and wine producers and entertainers in the gardens of the mansion. At Queenscliff *(above)* the streets are packed during the Spring Music Festival.

Previous pages: Darren Dickson shapes surfboards at Pure Glass Surfboards in Torquay. Bollards *(left)*, normally used for securing boats, have been turned into Geelong characters by Jan Mitchell. These are reminders of the beauty competitions that were held on the beach front from the 1930s. The shipping channels of Port Phillip Bay *(below)* are narrow, and come very close to the beach at Point Lonsdale.

The Torquay coast from the air *(left)* gives a hint of what makes surfing here so special. The Bellarine Peninsula hosts many international competitions, from the Bell's Beach Classic surf event, recognised as the world's oldest surfing competition, to the Spray Farm spring equestrian festival *(above)*.

The beach at Point Lonsdale is wide, even when the tide is in. When it's out, there's a long way to wade for a good swim, which makes it a favoured beach for families with young children.

CHAPTER FIVE

MACEDON AND SUNBURY

One of Victoria's smallest wine regions, Sunbury makes up for its size by its versatility. Located beyond the Tullamarine airport, about half an hour's drive northwest from Melbourne, it is one of the city's dormitory suburbs. It is also a farming district. Victoria's first homestead is at Emu Bottom and the birthplace of cricket's Ashes is at Rupertswood

Sunbury is situated in a little rain shadow, so it is dry country around here. Good for sheep. And in a neat twist of gastronomic good fortune, where there are good sheep in Victoria, there will often be good shiraz. It is like companion planting for the table, since lamb and shiraz suit each other so well. However, in the fickle nature of primary industry, they are unlikely to be equally valuable at any one time. Pat Carmody, winemaker of Craiglee in Sunbury, remembers one particular year when his father sent sheep off to market from the family property. Offered a gloomily low price, which he accepted, the senior Carmody shook his head and remarked: "The country's

The Forest Glade gardens *(left)* at Mount Macedon are open to the public and are at their multi-coloured best in autumn. A gargoyle *(below)* defends the gardens at Glen Rannach.

stuffed when a truck-load of sheep is worth less than two cases of wine."

Craiglee shiraz is one of Victoria's benchmark wines. The original Craiglee vineyard had first been planted in 1859, but was abandoned in the late 1920s. During its heyday, its hermitage (as shiraz was then known) was by all accounts an excellent wine. When some was discovered in an old cellar one of these legendary wines came out for re-assessment a century after it was made. As Pat Carmody tells it: "John Brown [of Brown Brothers] tasted the 1872 in 1972, and advised me to plant shiraz because any area that could produce a wine that still had fruit [flavours] after a century had to be a reasonable site."

Reasonable? That's characteristic of Pat Carmody's down-beat approach. These are not reasonably good wines, these are consistently wonderful wines. The shiraz is intense and spicy with fruit flavours that can—as demonstrated—maintain their character for at least a hundred years. There is nothing wrong with the chardonnay or cabernet sauvignon either. Even Craiglee's olives produce a fine nutty oil.

There are now about a dozen vineyards in the Sunbury wine area. Goona Warra is one of the most historic properties, even using its original

19th-century label design, while Wildwood at Bulla, closest to the airport, is one of the newer. There are some large plantings, but to date, this has been limited—partly because of water availability.

Twenty minutes along the highway, in the Macedon area, water is not a problem, but site selection is still crucial. Macedon is high and cool. On the wrong piece of earth, grapes will scarcely ripen. In the right places, there is the potential for good cool climate wines—sparkling wine in particular.

Macedon gives its name to a township, a mountain range and its highest peak. Mount Macedon was named after Phillip of Macedonia by the explorer Major Mitchell, who glimpsed Port Phillip Bay and the new settlement of Melbourne from the summit in 1836. Mitchell, who had found an overland trail to Melbourne from New South Wales, is best remembered for giving his name to the Major Mitchell pink-and-grey cockatoo.

Mount Macedon, 65 kilometres northwest of Melbourne, is garden country. Not pretty cottage gardens (although there are some of those), but immense landscaped affairs with rhododendrons as tall as oak trees. The wealthy of Melbourne usually go to Portsea on the Mornington Peninsula, but rich garden-lovers prefer to live in, or retire to, Mount Macedon. Its cooler climate provides welcome relief from the hot summers of the city.

Climate is the key word. Melbourne has weather (its variability being a standard joke), but this area has climate, with four distinct European-style seasons: cold winters, sometimes with snow, fluorescent green springs and multi-coloured summers and autumns. The great gardens here include Forest Glade, always open to the public. And they included others that were reduced to ashes in the bushfires of 1983. Also burnt in those fires were giant old trees that had been raised from seed supplied by Ferdinand von Mueller, the government botanist from 1853 to 1896. The flames are now

John Ellis of Hanging Rock Winery watches some old-fashioned pigeage, a procedure designed to crush grapes in a way that encourages long slow fermentation.

more likely to be contained in an open fire in one of the many bed-and-breakfasts, warming those who come here for cosy wintry getaways.

For vineyards, it's all about site, right through the Macedon area. Straws Lane produces gewürztraminer and pinot noir. There's excellent riesling and shiraz from Knight's Granite Hills at Kyneton, and supple pinot from Rochford at Romsey.

When Alec Epis, one of the great stars of the Essendon football club, bought land at cool Woodend in 1980, his wine friends recommended planting pinot noir. He was reluctant. "I don't want wimpy wine," he grumbled.

For him, wine was part of the life he had always known. "I'm Italian," he says, as if it explains everything. His grandfather had come from northern Italy and had gone into gold mining at distant Kalgoorlie, in Western Australia. Even there, the family grew their own vegetables. At Woodend, Alec Epis makes his own bread, cures his own olives, cheese and hams, and strikes his own roses. His pinot noir, made by Stuart Anderson, a musician and gifted winemaker, is dark, intense, savoury and aromatic.

"People say pinot noir is difficult," he says. "It's not. It's only difficult if you haven't got the right site, and if you over-crop."

His crop levels are low—only one and a half tonnes to the acre, even for the chardonnay and the cabernet sauvignon grown at his Kyneton vineyards. And, as many successful small vignerons do, he sells his wine by mail order or at

The vineyards at Hanging Rock winery are part of an extensive operation that includes a wide range of wines and styles, a cellar door, and accommodation for wine-tourists in self-contained units.

Vineyard dogs are a special breed. This one is pictured with his winemaker owner, Llew Knight of Granite Hills near Kyneton. The boulders through the landscape on the way to the winery explain the name, but do not forecast the quality of the riesling and the shiraz.

cellar door. Limited production, limited market, and a sell-out.

But for others, like John and Ann Ellis at Hanging Rock Winery, making and selling is big business. At their winery, the largest in the area, the cellar door is open daily. The Ellises are known Australia-wide. John Ellis is a judge at wine shows and a key figure in industry organisations. They make some wines from their Hanging Rock vineyards and source grapes from other areas, producing a range wide enough for a whole year of drinking. This is not a modest choice of pinot noir or chardonnay, but an extensive selection at various pricing levels of sparkling wine, sauvignon blanc, chardonnay, cabernet sauvignon, shiraz and pinot noir.

The Macedon area showed its potential for sparkling wines early on. But what were they to be called? World trade agreements supported the French in their insistence that champagne was the name for the sparkling wine produced in the geographical area of the same name. So what to call bubbly from the Macedon area? The Ellises opted for Macedon Sparkling. Gordon Cope-Williams chose Romsey. In addition, the Ellises have also demonstrated another possibility for the area by producing their multi-award-winning Jim Jim sauvignon blanc.

Hanging Rock, a rare rock formation, has been a nature reserve and a great tourist attraction for more than a century. It achieved cinematic stardom when Joan Lindsay's novel about Victorian schoolgirls who disappeared there on an excursion became the movie *Picnic at Hanging Rock*. Picnics in the reserve are popular, as they always were, even before the girls in the long white cotton dresses came to fictional grief. But so is climbing, walking and the New Year's Day race meeting. At the Harvest Picnic Festival at the end of February each year, thousands of visitors arrive with their baskets and picnic rugs for a day of sampling Victorian wine and food.

Macedon markets itself as a region with what is known as Spa Country further to the west. Hepburn Springs and Daylesford have the largest mineral springs in Australia, and at the former is a major hydrotherapy centre. There are few vines around here, but every other indulgence comes in abundance.

Spa Country was settled early on by Swiss-Italians, who planted the vast pine trees that still scent the air. The pines are controversial (their opponents want to restore native vegetation), but everything else has been revived. The pasta factory has re-opened, the local bullboar sausages are still made by butchers, and stone cottages have been given a new lease of life. There's even a Swiss-Italian Festa at Hepburn Springs every year.

This is the weekend-away capital, with dozens of cottages and bed-and-breakfast places. Once upon a time there was gold in the hills; now the old miners' cottages have been turned into getaways, along with guesthouses, hotels and inns.

The area has been transformed. Among those responsible are Alla and Allan Wolf-Tasker who began the Lake House as a small weekend-only restaurant (bring-your-own-wine) about 20 years ago. Alla was spurred on by her childhood memories of holidaying at Daylesford with her parents who came for the waters, as European-born parents did in the 1950s and 1960s. When the Wolf-Taskers started business, Daylesford was poor with high unemployment. Now it's a busy haven for food-lovers, book-lovers, artists, antique-hunters and walkers.

Food matters for the people around here. Trentham is a major potato-growing area. There are berry farms (raspberries are particularly good), honey, vegetable and herb gardens, orchards, ducks and chickens. Much of the produce is sold at roadside stalls and local markets, such as the Sunday market at the Daylesford railway station.

Kyneton is at the northern end of the Macedon wine region. It is a solid and impressive town, a mixture of colonial bluestone buildings, gardens that feature massed daffodils in spring and, of course, vineyards. The area is certainly a green and leafy region. It is all about sites, as they say around here. And, what makes Sunbury and Macedon so rewarding is that there is a site for every purpose.

Pat Carmody and his wife Diane pick sauvignon blanc grapes from the back block at Craiglee. The vineyard is renowned for its shiraz, which is unusually long-lived.

There is a good life after great football. Former Essendon star player, Alec Epis *(left)* divides his time between Melbourne and his Woodend vineyard, where he grows pinot noir, chardonnay and roses, cures his own olives, makes cheese, and bakes bread. How do you make a wombat? One way is to start with two wombats, but it's probably easier when Daylesford artist Miriam Porter *(above)* takes a chainsaw to timber.

They were both teachers when they met, and she cooked and he painted. Together Alla Wolf-Tasker and her husband Allan have created a remarkable enterprise in the Lake House at Daylesford, built around an award-winning restaurant with resort and conference facilities.

Al fresco dining at La Trattoria restaurant *(above)* at Lavandula, a former Swiss-Italian farmhouse turned lavender farm, located outside Daylesford. Built in the 1860's, the Convent Gallery at Daylesford *(right)* is a now a major tourist attraction with an extensive art and craft gallery as well as a popular café.

More than a grand building, Rupertswood has a special place in the hearts of cricket fans. This is where the sporting trophy "the Ashes" originated. Now a conference venue and reception centre, Rupertswood is an impressive example of 19th-century Victorian architecture. The stained-glass windows *(above)* give an account of a gentleman's (and gentlewoman's) life at the time.

The green of the Craiglee vineyards above, contrasts with the characteristic tawny gold of the dry countryside north of Macedon on the right.

The Daylesford-Hepburn Springs area is water country, with mineral springs, lakes and falls that provide water for hydrotherapy and make it great walking territory. Trentham Falls *(left)* is said to be the highest waterfall in Victoria. Sanitorium Lake *(above)* at Mount Macedon, was named after the tuberculosis sanatorium built in 1899 and closed in 1910. Hanging Rock *(following pages)* was the star of the movie that signalled a renaissance for the Australian film industry.

SUGGESTED READING

Yarra Valley Wineguide, *by Max Allen, published by Pizzey WIF*

A Concise History of Australian Wine, *by John Beeston, published by Allen & Unwin*

Journey to Wine in Victoria, *by W. S.Benwell, published by Pitman Publishing*

The Australian Vegetable Garden, *by Clive Blazey, published by New Holland Publishing*

John Bull's Vineyard, Australian Sketches *by Hubert de Castella, first published by Sands & McDougall*

The Land Boomers, *by Michael Cannon, published by Lloyd O'Neil*

The Art of the Boyds, *by Patricia Dobrez & Peter Herbst, published by Bay Books*

Better than Pommard, A History of Wine in Victoria, *by David Dunstan, published by Australian Scholarly Publishing & The Museum of Victoria*

Introduction to the Life and Adventures of William Buckley, *by Tim Flannery, published by Text Publishing*

The Chronicle of Early Melbourne, *by Garry Owen, published by Heritage Publications*

The French Presence in Victoria 1800-1901, *published by Alliance Francaise de Melbourne*

Picnic at Hanging Rock, *by Joan Lindsay, published by Penguin*

Surfing Victoria, *by Richard Loveridge, published by Phillip Mathews*

A History of the Port Phillip District, *by A. G. L. Shaw, published by Miegunyah Press*

The Vineyards of Victoria, as Visited by Ebenezer Ward in 1864, *published by Sullivan's Cove*

When the Wattles Bloom Again: The Life and Times of William Barak, Last Chief of the Yarra Yarra Tribe, *by Shirley Wiencke, published by Woori Yallock*

Barrabool Land of the Magpie, *by Ian Wynd, published by Barrabool Shire*

The Artists Retreat: Discovering the Mornington Peninsula 1850s To The Present, *published by Mornington Peninsula Regional Gallery*

ACKNOWLEDGMENTS

The photographer and writer would like to thank the following for their generous help in the preparation of this book: Stuart Anderson, Clive Blazey, Clive Callaway, Pat Carmody, Tom Carson, Laura Cavallo, Paul Chambers, Chris Ciastkowski, Dianne Clarke, Guill de Pury, John Dent, Tod Dexter, Darren Dickson, Ross Ebbels, Reg Egan, Maryann Egan, John & Anne Ellis, Alec Epis, Caroline Evans, Gary Farr, Peter Fergusson, Janet & Mike Green, James Halliday, Suzanne Halliday, Nicole Issac-Griggs, Dr. Tony Jordan, Llew Knight, Rob Knottenbelt, George Kuruvilla, Dr. Peter McMahon, Ian Marks, Richard McIntyre, Dr. John Middleton, Jan Mitchell, Sue O'Brien, Michael O'Connor, Jeremy Oliver, Miriam Porter, Julia Portet, Jack Rasterhoff, Andrew Riddell, David Ridley, Kiff Saunders, Rachel Scicluna, Richard Shenfield, Julie & Jim Staddon, Nadège Suné, Christine Turner, Christina Turner, Alex White, Carol White, David Williams, Alla & Allan Wolf-Tasker and Will Wolseley.

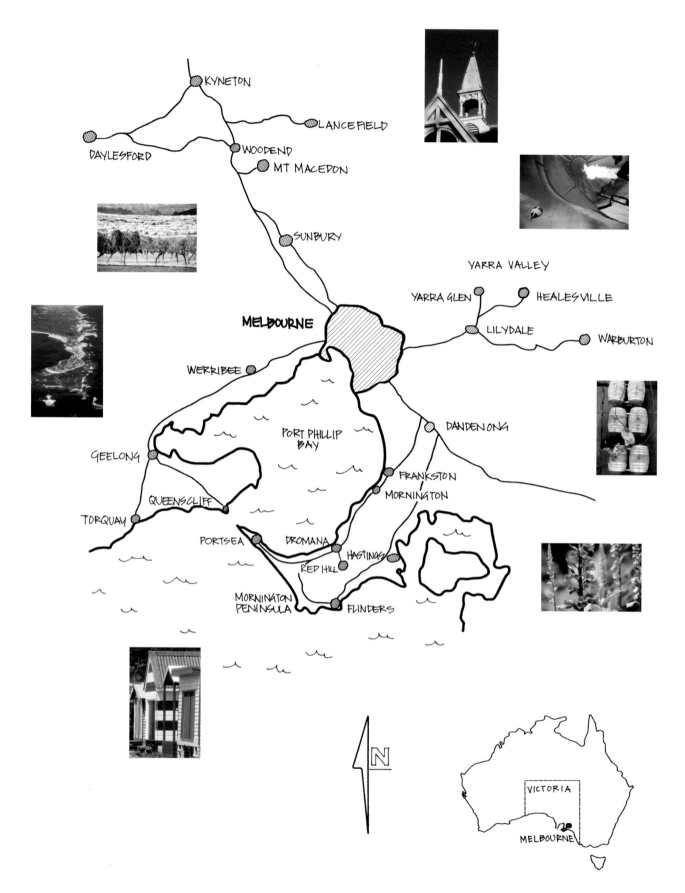

KYNETON

LANCEFIELD

DAYLESFORD

WOODEND

MT MACEDON

SUNBURY

YARRA VALLEY

YARRA GLEN   HEALESVILLE

MELBOURNE

LILYDALE   WARBURTON

WERRIBEE

DANDENONG

PORT PHILLIP BAY

GEELONG

FRANKSTON

MORNINGTON

QUEENSCLIFF

TORQUAY

PORTSEA   DROMANA

HASTINGS

RED HILL

MORNINGTON PENINSULA   FLINDERS

N

VICTORIA

MELBOURNE

Photography by: R. Ian Lloyd
Text by: Rita Erlich
Edited by: Wendy Moore
Layout: Canopy Design
Series Design : Yolanta Woldendorp

Around Melbourne – Travelling Australia's Wine
Regions was first published in 2002 by:
R. Ian Lloyd Productions Pte Ltd
5 Kreta Ayer Road, Singapore 088983
Tel: (65) 6227-9600 Fax: (65) 6227-9363
Email: library@rianlloyd.com.sg
Website: http://www.rianlloyd.com.sg

Historical photos on pages 12, 18, 19 & 20
are reproduced with the kind permission of the
Museum of Lillydale.
The following are reproduced with the permission
of the National Library of Australia.
Page 14: The Blair watercolour
Page 15: S.T. Gill watercolour
Page 16: Robert Bruce engraving
Page 17: The Cerberus off Geelong
Page 21: Victorian Railways poster by
          James Northfield

Map on Page 144 by Kevin Sloan.

This book is available for bulk purchase for sales
promotion and premium use from
R. Ian Lloyd Productions Pte Ltd

Distributed in Australia by:
Tower Books Australia
PO Box 213, Brookvale
NSW, 2100, Australia
Phone: (61) 2 9975 5566
Fax: (61) 2 9975 5599

Printed in Singapore using the computer to plate
process by Tien Wah Press Pte Ltd
ISBN No. 981-04-6588-2
10 9 8 7 6 5 4 3 2 1